GETTING BETTER ALL THE TIME

HOW TO CONTROL IMPULSES

BY GOLRIZ GOLKAR

TIPS FOR CAREGIVERS

Social and emotional learning (SEL) helps children manage emotions, create and achieve goals, maintain relationships, learn how to feel empathy, and make good decisions. The SEL approach will help children establish positive habits in communication, cooperation, and decision-making. By incorporating SEL in early reading, children will be better equipped to build confidence and foster positive peer networks.

BEFORE READING

Talk to the reader about times people might act without thinking first.

Discuss: Think of a time you did something suddenly without thinking it through beforehand. What did you do? What happened right after? How did you feel?

AFTER READING

Talk to the reader about different ways to control their impulses.

Discuss: What can you do when you feel an impulse? How can controlling your impulses help you manage your feelings?

SEL GOAL

Impulses can make it difficult to make good decisions. Giving in to impulses can affect others. Have students work in groups of three and think of an impulsive scenario they can act out together. One student should have the impulse, one should be affected by the behavior, and one should offer a solution. Have them discuss how controlling the impulse helps everyone.

TABLE OF CONTENTS

CHAPTER 1
What Are Impulses? 4

CHAPTER 2
What You Can Do 6

CHAPTER 3
Good Decisions 16

GOALS AND TOOLS
Grow with Goals 22
Try This! 22
Glossary 23
To Learn More 23
Index 24

CHAPTER 1

WHAT ARE IMPULSES?

Greg eats one cookie. He wants more, but he got a stomachache the last time he ate too many. Greg stops himself.

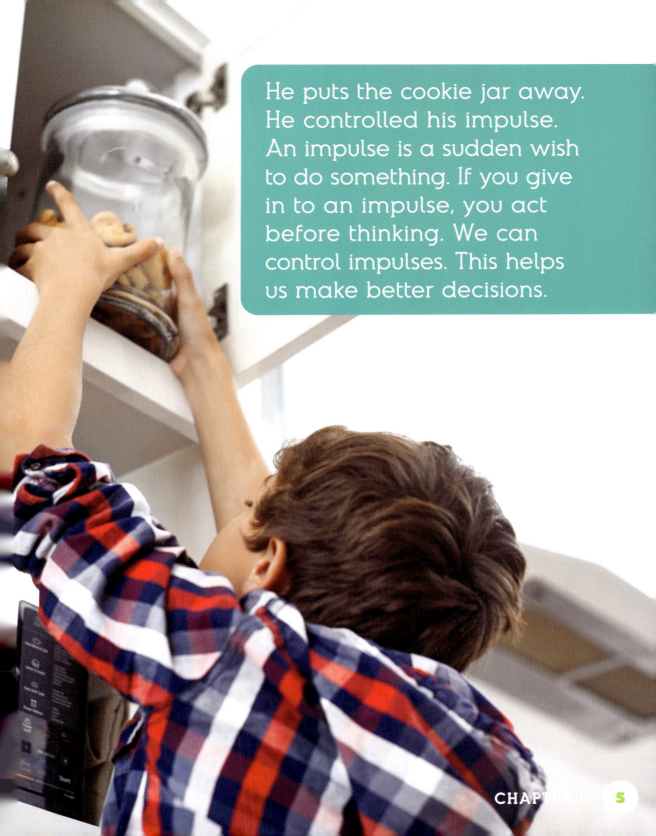

He puts the cookie jar away. He controlled his impulse. An impulse is a sudden wish to do something. If you give in to an impulse, you act before thinking. We can control impulses. This helps us make better decisions.

CHAPTER 2

WHAT YOU CAN DO

Strong emotions may lead to impulses. For example, anger can make you want to scream or say something mean. If you are **annoyed**, you might stick out your tongue at someone. Acting on impulses might not be nice or safe.

When you feel an impulse, imagine a stop sign. Think about how your impulse could affect you and others. Ask yourself, "Is this a good idea? What will happen if I act on my impulse?" Then make the best decision.

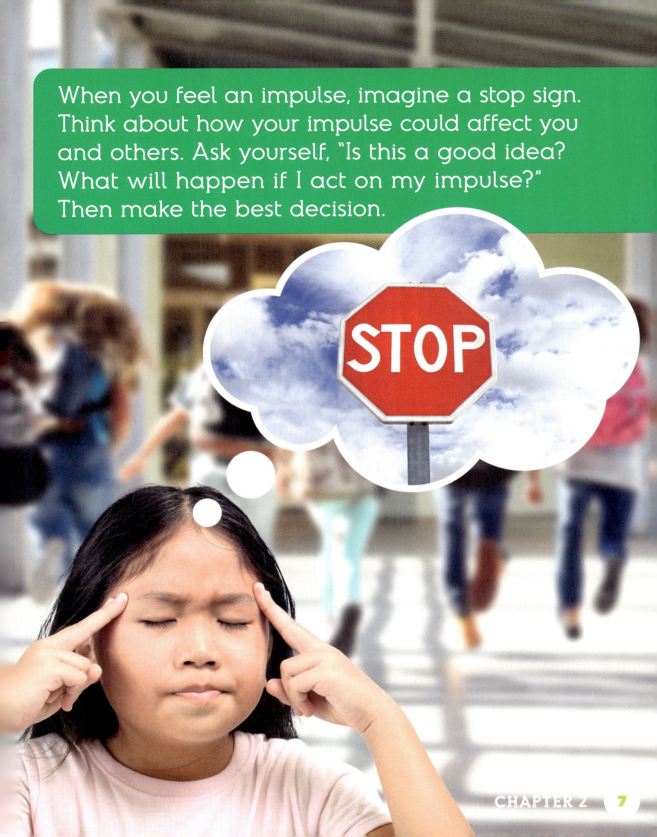

CHAPTER 2　7

Kenny's teacher asks a question. Kenny knows the answer! He wants to shout it out. But other students are raising their hands. Kenny realizes shouting out the answer is rude. Others are waiting their turn. Kenny raises his hand instead.

BE SELF-AWARE

Being **self-aware** can help you learn to control impulses. Pay attention to your actions. What happens after? How do others **react**? Noticing these things can help you decide how to act next time you are in a similar situation.

CHAPTER 2

You can control impulses by moving your body in healthy, safe ways. Dancing, jump roping, or stretching can **distract** your thoughts. Movement can get rid of **stress** and anger. It can help clear your mind so you can make good decisions.

> ### GAME TIME
> Games such as "Red Light, Green Light," "Simon Says," and freeze dancing can help you control impulses. How? They teach you to be patient, follow rules, and think before you act.

CHAPTER 2

CHAPTER 2

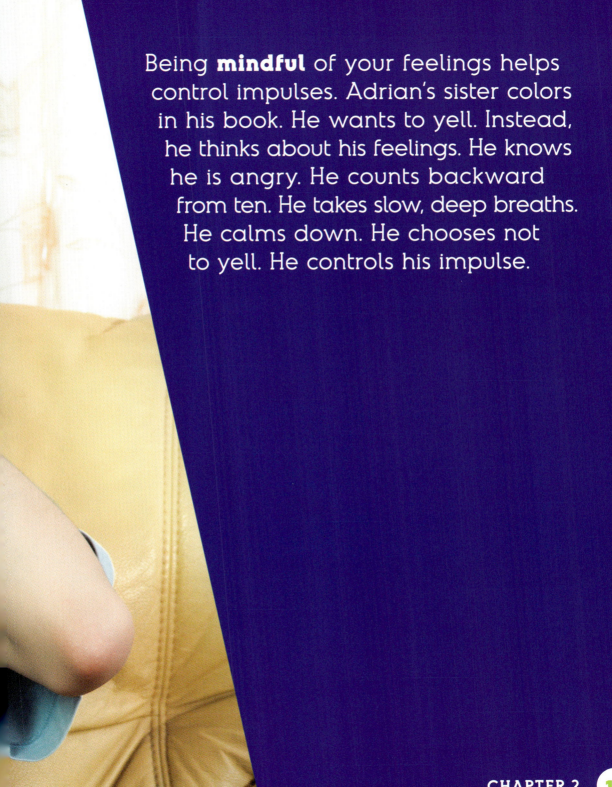

Being **mindful** of your feelings helps control impulses. Adrian's sister colors in his book. He wants to yell. Instead, he thinks about his feelings. He knows he is angry. He counts backward from ten. He takes slow, deep breaths. He calms down. He chooses not to yell. He controls his impulse.

CHAPTER 2

Dana is on her phone. Her mom says it is time for dinner. Dana is annoyed. She wants to slam the door shut so she cannot hear her mom. Instead, Dana closes her eyes and **meditates**. She pictures her mom. Dana knows acting on her impulse would hurt her mom's feelings. She puts her phone away. She goes downstairs for dinner.

PICTURE THIS

Picturing something you like can help you fight an impulse. It changes your thoughts to something positive. This helps calm you down. You can then make a good decision.

14 CHAPTER 2

CHAPTER 2

CHAPTER 3

GOOD DECISIONS

When you control an impulse, you think first. This helps you make good decisions. It helps you get along better with others.

Will and Johnny build a model ship. Johnny makes a mistake. Will wants to finish building by himself. But he stops to think. He does not want to hurt Johnny's feelings. He thinks about how he would feel if Johnny finished the model without him. He decides to help him instead.

CHAPTER 3

Laura wants to be the first to finish a math test. But the last time she worked quickly, she made mistakes. She closes her eyes and pictures a good grade. She slows down and works carefully. Laura does well on the test.

CHAPTER 3

Aaron broke his mom's vase. He is nervous. Should he lie and say the dog did it? Lying will make his mom upset. Aaron tells the truth. His mom tells Aaron that honesty helps people understand and respect each other. Aaron is **relieved** he told the truth.

With practice, you can learn to control your impulses. It will help you make better decisions and get along better with others.

CHAPTER 3 21

GOALS AND TOOLS

GROW WITH GOALS

Learning to control impulses takes practice. The more you practice, the easier it gets! Try following these goals:

Goal: Write down emotions that make you feel impulses. Then write what might happen if you don't control the impulses. Come up with solutions for controlling your impulses.

Goal: Make a list of things that make you happy. Write them down. Read them when you feel an impulse.

Goal: Think of different rules at school, home, or in the community that keep people safe and help them control impulses. Make a chart with two columns. List each rule in the left column, and write down why the rule is important in the right column.

TRY THIS!

Try these steps the next time you have an impulse:

1. Think about what emotion is causing the impulse.

2. What might happen if you act on your impulse? Ask: "Is this a good decision? Will it cause problems for other people or myself?"

3. Think of one way to control it. What makes the most sense for that impulse? Could you get up and do a physical activity? Or would it be best to take deep breaths and picture something in your mind?

GLOSSARY

annoyed
Feeling angry or irritated.

distract
To weaken your focus on what you are doing.

meditates
Thinks deeply and quietly as a way of relaxing the mind and body.

mindful
A mentality achieved by focusing on the present moment and calmly recognizing and accepting your feelings, thoughts, and sensations.

react
To behave in a particular way as a response to something that has happened.

relieved
No longer being upset or weighed down by something.

self-aware
Knowing your feelings.

stress
Mental or emotional strain or pressure.

TO LEARN MORE

Finding more information is as easy as 1, 2, 3.

1. Go to www.factsurfer.com
2. Enter "**howtocontrolimpulses**" into the search box.
3. Choose your book to see a list of websites.

GOALS AND TOOLS   23

INDEX

act 5, 6, 7, 9, 10, 14

anger 6, 10, 13

annoyed 6, 14

decisions 5, 7, 10, 14, 16, 20

deep breaths 13

games 10

get along 16, 20

lying 20

meditates 14

mindful 13

movement 10

nervous 20

patient 10

react 9

relieved 20

rules 10

self-aware 9

stops 4, 7, 17

stress 10

truth 20

Blue Owl Books are published by Jump!, 3500 American Blvd W, Suite 150, Bloomington, MN 55431, www.jumplibrary.com

Copyright © 2026 Jump! International copyright reserved in all countries. No part of this book may be reproduced in any form without written permission from the publisher.

Jump! is a division of FlutterBee Education Group.

Library of Congress Cataloging-in-Publication Data

Names: Golkar, Golriz, author.
Title: How to control impulses / by Golriz Golkar.
Description: Minneapolis, MN: Jump!, Inc., [2026]
Series: Getting better all the time | Includes index.
Audience: Ages 7–10
Identifiers: LCCN 2025001262 (print)
LCCN 2025001263 (ebook)
ISBN 9798892138857 (hardcover)
ISBN 9798892138864 (paperback)
ISBN 9798892138871 (ebook)
Subjects: LCSH: Impulse–Juvenile literature. | Social learning–Juvenile literature.
Classification: LCC BF575.I46 G65 2026 (print)
LCC BF575.I46 (ebook)
DDC 303.3/2–dc23/eng/20250212
LC record available at https://lccn.loc.gov/2025001262
LC ebook record available at https://lccn.loc.gov/2025001263

Editor: Alyssa Sorenson
Designer: Molly Ballanger
Content Consultant: Lisa Meyers, PhD, LCSW

Photo Credits: nednapa/Shutterstock, cover (tablet); NextMarsMedia/Shutterstock, cover (game); hartphotography/Shutterstock, 1; ViJpeg/Shutterstock, 3; PeopleImages - Yuri A/Shutterstock, 4, 5; kwanchai.c/Shutterstock, 6, 7 (girl); WINDCOLORS/Shutterstock, 7 (sign); Monkey Business Images/Shutterstock, 7 (background); nimito/Adobe Stock, 8–9; Vibe Images/Adobe Stock, 10–11; Morakod1977/Shutterstock, 12–13; fizkes/Shutterstock, 14–15; LattaPictures/iStock, 16; romrodinka/iStock, 17; Ridofranz/iStock, 18–19; dezign56/Shutterstock, 20; triloks/iStock, 20–21.

Printed in the United States of America at Corporate Graphics in North Mankato, Minnesota.

24 GOALS AND TOOLS